Millie Marotta's
Animal
Adventures

T0347707

First published in the United Kingdom
in 2023 by
B. T. Batsford Ltd
43 Great Ormond Street
London
WC1N 3HZ

An imprint of B. T. Batsford Holdings Limited

ISBN 978 1 84994 843 2

A CIP catalogue record for this book is available
from the British Library.

10 9 8 7 6 5 4 3 2 1

Reproduction by Mission Productions, Hong Kong
Printed in Malaysia

This book can be ordered direct from the publisher at www.batsfordbooks.com,
or try your local bookshop

FSC
www.fsc.org

MIX
Paper from
responsible sources
FSC® C084469

Millie Marotta's
Animal Adventures

Favourite illustrations from
seas, forests and islands

BATSFORD

Introduction

Art and nature are truly a match made in heaven; I can't think of a better way to spend my days than creating my books, which allow me to indulge in my two passions. And one of the absolute best things – after many months of researching, planning, sketching and inking – is that once a book is finally out there in the world, I get to see the coloured pages begin to trickle into my colouring gallery. It's remarkable to see the brilliant ways that different colourists approach the same image, resulting in pages that are as unique as their creators. It's also incredibly inspiring to collaborate with such a talented community: the novelty of seeing my black-and-white line drawings brought to life in so many different ways never wears off.

Seeing which drawings people go for first when a new book is released, those that jump out and shout, 'Colour me!', is always fascinating. And as more coloured pages appear, it becomes clear that there are firm favourites. Some people love sprawling botanicals, while others delight in the simplicity of a single flower. There are those who relish mindbogglingly detailed mandalas while others enjoy a simple animal portrait.

Animal Adventures brings together those most popular illustrations from my last three books; *Woodland Wild*, *Secrets of The Sea* and *Island Escape* – a 'greatest hits' if you like; a curated collection of the colouring community's favourites. These are the drawings that have something irresistible about them to curious colourists. If you haven't yet delved into those three books, then *Animal Adventures* is a great place to get a taste of each. And as a sneaky surprise, dotted among the pages, you'll find a sprinkling of brand-new illustrations, exclusive to this collection.

Of course I have my own favourites, and I often have a good sense of which might end up being popular, but there are some pages that take me completely by surprise. Not all of the drawings come easy. Some come together quickly in a flash of inspiration, but others can take much longer and might exist in many different sketch forms before I finally settle on the chosen one. Even then, I might not feel completely confident about them. But to my surprise, sometimes those are the very ones that turn out to be the stars of the show.

Bringing together a selection of images like this creates a wonderful assortment of animals to explore, from habitats all over the globe. As you flick through the pages, you'll find unlikely partners; a humpback whale in the company of a hoopoe, comet moths sharing space with a seahorse or a three-toed sloth starring alongside an Atlantic puffin. Each new book introduces me to species I didn't know existed, and I explore these with the wide-eyed wonderment that I've always had for our natural world. I hope that in turn, it can do the same for you. The glossary at the back tells you what species you are colouring, not just so you can find out what colours they are in real life but also for you to learn about the creatures themselves, many of which are in need of our help and protection as they become increasingly threatened by habitat destruction, illegal hunting, climate change and other environmental factors. I create colouring books to champion the idea that anyone can be creative, but it's also my hope that my illustrations will pique your curiosity for the natural world. And whatever your colouring crush is – maybe you're a sucker for pretty pastels or crazy for clashing colour combos, love a luminous palette or hanker for harmonious hues – *Animal Adventures* will have your colouring tastebuds truly tantalised!

So, the time has come to begin your animal adventures. Dive deep beneath the oceans, meander through towering trees or get set for a spot of island-hopping as you journey across the continents, bringing colourful life to an extraordinary array of species.

Millie Marotta

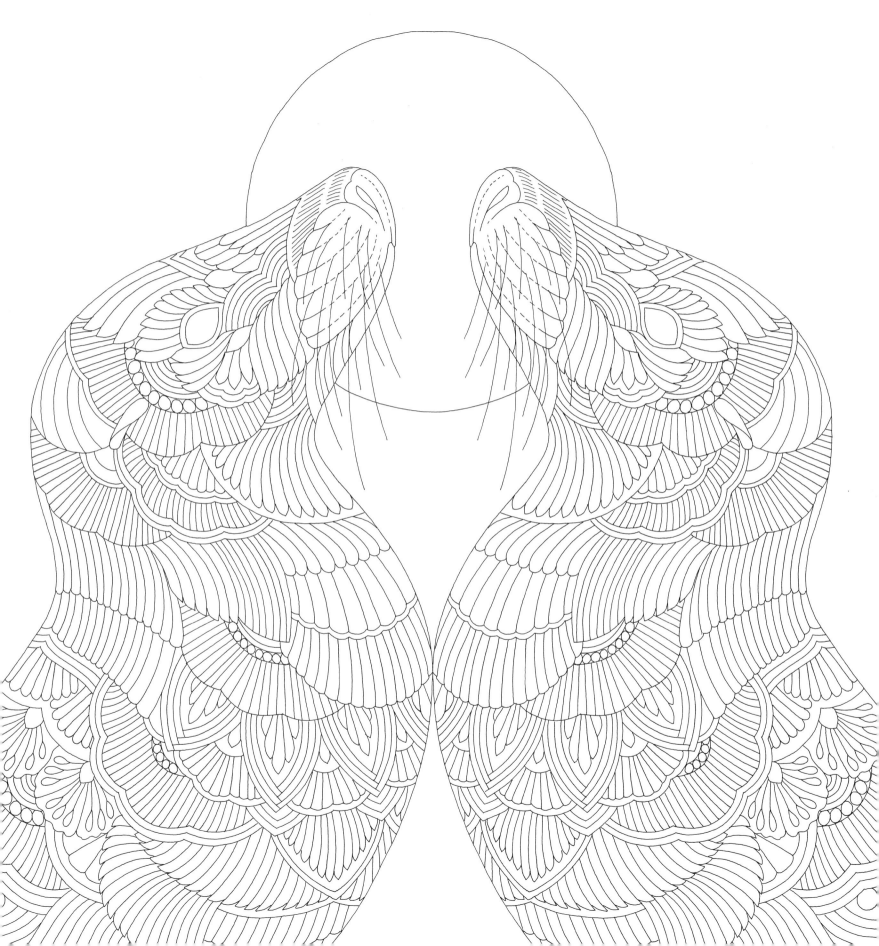

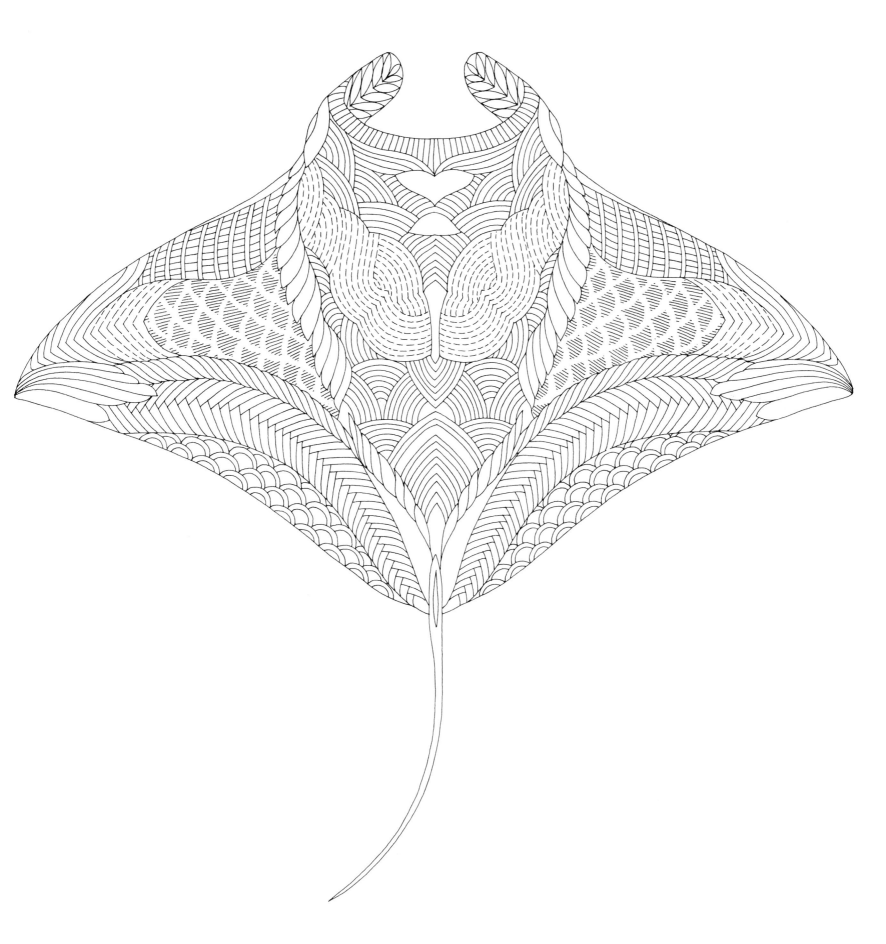

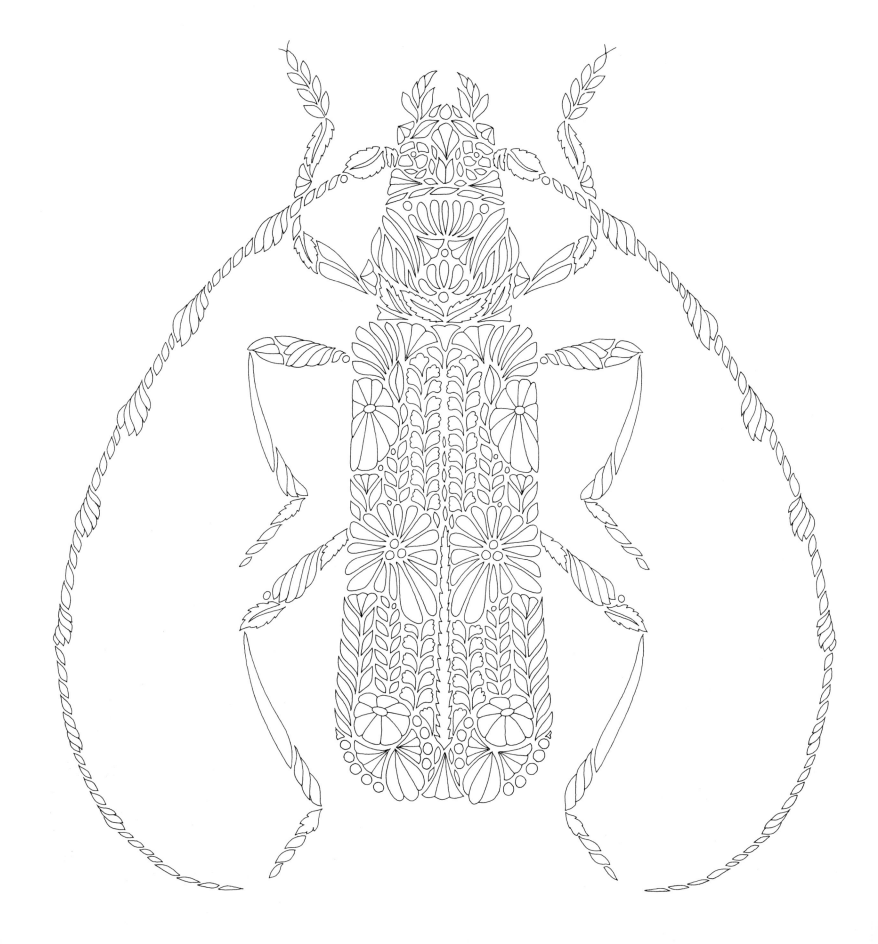

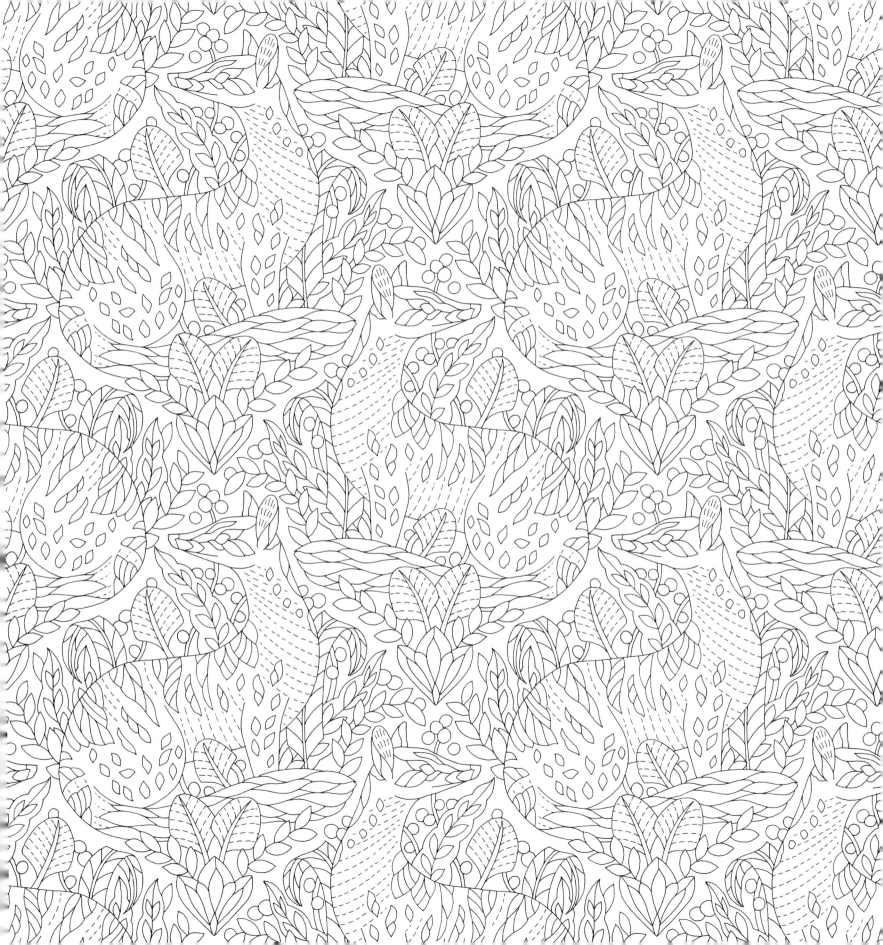

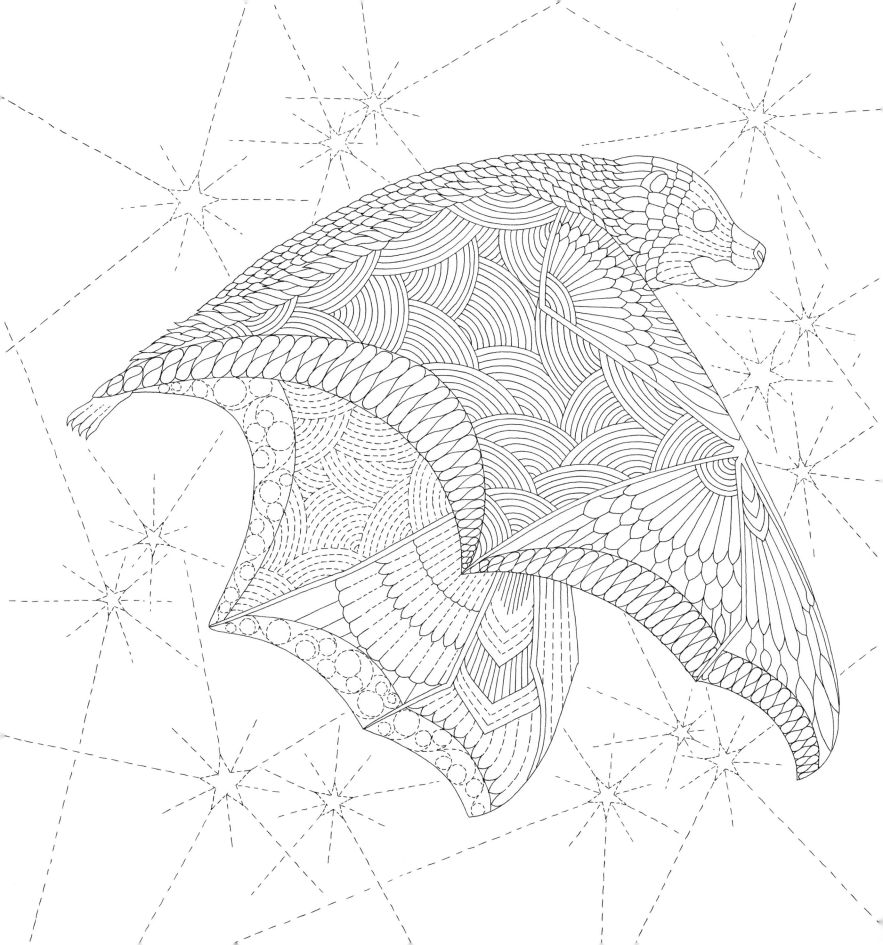

List of creatures in Animal Adventures

Common octopus
  (*Octopus vulgaris*)
Purple emperor butterfly
  (*Apatura iris*)
Antillean palm swift
  (*Tachornis phoenicobia*)
Vaquita
  (*Phocoena sinus*)
Red-tailed tropicbird
  (*Phaethon rubricauda*)
European hedgehog
  (*Erinaceus europaeus*)
Floreana mockingbird
  (*Mimus trifasciatus*) and Galápagos
  prickly pear (*Opuntia galapageia*)
Sea otters
  (*Enhydra lutris*)
European badger
  (*Meles meles*)
African wild dog
  (*Lycaon pictus*)
Saucer magnolia
  (*Magnolia* x *soulangeana*) and long-
  tailed tits (*Aegithalos caudatus*)
Icon star
  (*Iconaster longimanus*)
Kakapo
  (*Strigops habroptilus*)
Javan rhinoceros
  (*Rhinoceros sondaicus*)

North American (West Indian)
  manatees (*Trichechus manatus*)
Saola
  (*Pseudoryx nghetinhensis*)
Japanese hare
  (*Lepus brachyurus*)
Walrus
  (*Odobenus rosmarus*)
Fallow deer
  (*Dama dama*)
Japanese pygmy woodpecker
  (*Yungipicus kizuki*) and Indian
  peafowl (*Pavo cristatus*)
Carola's parotia
  (*Parotia carolae*)
Northern sea robin
  (*Prionotus carolinus*)
European goldfinches
  (*Carduelis carduelis*) and
  hazel catkins (*Corylus avellana*)
Borneo pygmy elephant
  (*Elephas maximus borneensis*)
Saltwater crocodiles
  (*Crocodylus porosus*)
O'ahu tree snail
  (*Achatinella mustelina*)
Comet moth
  (*Argema mittrei*)
Thorny (spiny) seahorse
  (*Hippocampus histrix*)

Ring-tailed lemur
  (*Lemur catta*)
Pittas
  Azure-breasted pitta (*Pitta steerii*)
  Black-faced pitta (*Pitta anerythra*)
  Superb pitta (*Pitta superba*)
  Whiskered pitta (*Erythropitta kochi*)
Pale green awlet
  (*Bibasis gomata*)
British Columbia wolf
  (*Canis lupus columbianus*)
Mariana fruit dove
  (*Ptilinopus roseicapilla*)
Emperor penguin
  (*Aptenodytes forsteri*)
Seahorses
  Pot-bellied seahorse
    (*Hippocampus abdominalis*)
  Slender (longsnout) seahorse
    (*Hippocampus reidi*)
  Tiger tail seahorse
    (*Hippocampus comes*)
  Lined (northern) seahorse
    (*Hippocampus erectus*)
Picasso bug
  (*Sphaerocoris annulus*)
Elk
  (*Cervus canadensis*)

Dragon blood tree
   (*Dracaena cinnabari*) and
      Socotran white-eye
   (*Zosterops socotranus*)
Galápagos sea lions
   (*Zalophus wollebaeki*)
Striped skunk
   (*Mephitis mephitis*)
Japanese serow
   (*Capricornis crispus*)
Narwhal
   (*Monodon monoceros*)
Common raven
   (*Corvus corax*)
Red-tail golden arowana
   (*Scleropages aureus*)
Scalloped hammerhead shark
   (*Sphyrna lewini*)
Alpine newt
   (*Ichthyosaura alpestris*)
Fishing cat
   (*Prionailurus viverrinus*)
Harlequin crab
   (*Lissocarcinus orbicularis*)
Eastern spinebill
   (*Acanthorhynchus tenuirostris*)
Pygmy three-toed sloth
   (*Bradypus pygmaeus*)
Atlantic puffin
   (*Fratercula arctica*)

Bengal tiger
   (*Panthera tigris tigris*)
Scilly bee
   (*Bombus muscorum var. scyllonius*)
Arctic tern
   (*Sterna paradisaea*)
Palmer's chipmunk
   (*Tamias palmeri*)
Ribbon-tailed astrapia
   (*Astrapia mayeri*)
Garden eels
   Splendid garden eel
      (*Gorgasia preclara*)
   Spotted garden eel
      (*Heteroconger hassi*)
   Galápagos garden eel
      (*Heteroconger klausewitzi*)
   Giraffe spotted garden eel
      (*Heteroconger camelopardalis*)
   Zebra garden eel
      (*Heteroconger polyzona*)
Skomer vole
   (*Myodes glareolus skomerensis*)
Japanese flying squid
   (*Todarodes pacificus*)
Red fox
   (*Vulpes vulpes*)
Bornean orangutan
   (*Pongo pygmaeus*)

Reef manta ray
   (*Mobula alfredi*)
Chinese water dragon
   (*Physignathus cocincinus*)
Cozumel or pygmy raccoon
   (*Procyon pygmaeus*)
Socotran chameleon
   (*Chamaeleo monachus*)
Sponges, coral and fish
   Sea goldie (*Pseudanthias squamipinnis*)
   Stove-pipe sponge (*Aplysina archeri*)
   Disc coral (*Turbinaria mesenterina*)
   Red coral (*Corallium rubrum*)
   Long sea whip (*Ellisella elongata*)
   Flowerpot coral
      (*Goniopora djiboutiensis*)
Rosalia longicorn beetle
   (*Rosalia alpina*)
Nine-banded armadillo
   (*Dasypus novemcinctus*)
Svalbard reindeer
   (*Rangifer tarandus platyrhynchus*)
Little auk
   (*Alle alle*)
Owston's palm civet
   (*Chrotogale owstoni*)
Humpback whale
   (*Megaptera novaeangliae*)
Eurasian hoopoe
   (*Upupa epops*)

Tufted pygmy squirrel
(*Exilisciurus whiteheadi*)
Ribbon eel
(*Rhinomuraena quaesita*)
Tree bumblebee
(*Bombus hypnorum*)
Yellow-bellied sunbird-asity
(*Neodrepanis hypoxantha*)
Polar bear
(*Ursus maritimus*)
Red-bordered stink bugs
(*Edessa rufomarginata*)
Mauritian flying fox
(*Pteropus niger*)
European shag
(*Phalacrocorax aristotelis*)
Splendid leaf frog
(*Cruziohyla calcarifer*)
Verreaux's sifaka
(*Propithecus verreauxi*)
Periwinkles
Rough periwinkle (*Littorina saxatilis*)
Flat periwinkle (*Littorina obtusata*)
Common periwinkle
(*Littorina littorea*)
Guyana toucanet
(*Selenidera piperivora*)
Andaman cobra
(*Naja sagittifera*)

Sea slugs
(*Chromodoris colemani,
Chromodoris roboi, Hypselodoris
bennetti, Hypselodoris maculosa*)
Peacock tarantula
(*Poecilotheria metallica*)
Sri Lankan junglefowl
(*Gallus lafayettii*)
European adder
(*Vipera berus*)
Sandhill crane
(*Antigone canadensis*)
Formosan rock macaque
(*Macaca cyclopis*)
European eel
(*Anguilla anguilla*)
Eurasian wren
(*Troglodytes troglodytes*)
Yellow-flanked fairy wrasse
(*Cirrhilabrus ryukyuensis*)
Tamaraw or Mindoro dwarf buffalo
(*Bubalus mindorensis*)
South Island takahe
(*Porphyrio hochstetteri*)
Fireflies
(*Photinus carolinus*)
Queen Alexandra's birdwing
(*Ornithoptera alexandrae*)
Inca tern
(*Larosterna inca*)

Kirk's dik-dik
(*Madoqua kirkii*)
Grey seal
(*Halichoerus grypus*)
Tsushima Island marten
(*Martes melampus tsuensis*)
Puffadder shyshark
(*Haploblepharus edwardsii*)
European rabbit
(*Oryctolagus cuniculus*)
Forktail blue-eye or forktail
rainbowfish (*Pseudomugil furcatus*)
Soft corals
(*from order Alcyonacea*)
Island darter
(*Sympetrum nigrifemur*)
Harlequin duck
(*Histrionicus histrionicus*)

Test your colour palettes and materials here…